A Picture History of the
AMERICA'S CUP

by John Rousmaniere

No trophy has seen continuous international competition longer than this bulbous, bottomless, 134-ounce silver ewer. It was called the "Squadron Cup" and the "Hundred Guinea Cup" when it was presented in 1851 to the winner of a 53-mile race organized by Britain's Royal Yacht Squadron. The race was won by the U.S. schooner *America*, and so the trophy came to be called "the *America* Cup" and, eventually, "the America's Cup."

Dedicated To
Stanley Rosenfeld,
master of shadow and light, seizer of moments

Most of the photographs in this book were taken by the Rosenfeld family, shown here in a portrait taken in 1954: (from left to right) David, Morris, Stanley, and William. Morris Rosenfeld took his first photo in the 1890's, covered his first America's Cup in 1920, and was active into the 1960's. His sons followed him into the profession, and Stanley made it his life's work. He shot his first Cup match in 1930, when he was 17, and covered the 1987 and 1988 races off Perth, Australia, and San Diego, California. In 1985, the Mystic Seaport Museum, in Mystic, Connecticut, purchased the family's collection of more than one million negatives and transparencies. Included in the Rosenfeld Collection are the works of other photographers in the period 1870-1910, some of which are published in these pages.

Acknowledgments

I thank Thomas Aageson, President of Mystic Seaport Museum Stores, for inviting me to take on this exciting and novel project. Donald G. Paulhus, the designer, and Joseph Gribbins, the editor, understood from the beginning what it was about. B.A.G. Fuller, Curator at Mystic Seaport Museum, was with us all along. Providing invaluable assistance while I searched through the Rosenfeld Collection were Elizabeth Parker Rafferty and her staff of professionals and volunteers, especially John MacFadyen and David Miller. Georgia York efficiently steered me through the catalogs at Mystic Seaport's Registrar's Office. Information about individual photographs was provided by Elizabeth Meyer, Elizabeth Morss, Stanley Rosenfeld, and Roderick Stephens Jr.

John Rousmaniere

Published by Mystic Seaport Museum Stores

© Copyright 1989 Text John Rousmaniere. All rights reserved.
No part of this publication may be duplicated without prior
written permission of the publisher.

Published simultaneously in English and Japanese.

Trade Edition distributed by W. W. Norton & Co.
Limited Edition of 975 copies by Christopher, Cabot & Fuller, Ltd., Atlanta, GA.

Edited by Joseph P. Gribbins

Designed by Donald G. Paulhus

Library of Congress Cataloging-in-Publication Data

Rousmaniere, John 1944 –
    A picture history of the America's Cup / by John Rousmaniere.
    Bibliography: p.
    1. America's Cup races – Pictorial works. I. Title.
    GV 829

Mystic Seaport Museum Stores, © 1989

ISBN 0-393-02819-4

Printed in Japan

Foreword

This is the first book to tell the 140-year story of the America's Cup in pictures selected from the rich archives of America's foremost maritime museum, Mystic Seaport, in Mystic, Connecticut. In choosing the nearly 200 illustrations printed here, I have tried to cover all the facets of that extraordinary history.

For too long, the Cup has been regarded as almost supernaturally aloof. In this view (represented by the famous photograph on page 47), huge yachts glide haughtily on the distant horizon. While this image of impersonal inaccessibility adds mystique, it is only a part of the story. People who watched the exciting races off Perth, Australia, on worldwide television were surprised to see that America's Cup racing has passion as well as majesty. This is the America's Cup shown in the action-packed photos on pages 104-107. The sweat of crews hauling on sheets, the absorption of skippers fighting wheels and wind, the boats thrashing through water and air in fierce bow-to-bow combat – all make this a sport for athletes as much as a pastime for the wealthy.

It's not commonly known that what many people discovered in 1987 actually has been true of the whole of America's Cup history. While the Cup has changed in some areas (for example, the length of the boats has ranged from 143 feet down to 60 feet), the fundamentals of Cup racing haven't altered much at all. For 140 years, some yachtsmen from one country have challenged some other yachtsmen from another country to a sailboat race, one boat against another, the winner to take home the same gaudy trophy that the schooner *America* won back in 1851. In Cup history, there have always been controversies, men with outsized egos and ambitions, and closely fought races. In short, there's not much that's new in America's Cup racing.

In tracing these themes, I have chosen to stroll – rather than march in lock step – down the chronological path of Cup history. Some photo essays highlight broad trends; for example, the five matches in the enormous gaff-rigged sloops of the Herreshoff era between 1893 and 1903 intermingle on pages 20-41. Other essays scrutinize specific events; for instance, on pages 66-73 there is a sequence of superb photographs of one of the most exciting of all Cup races.

The worst part in choosing these pictures was that I had to reject ten times as many as I chose. Inevitably, some of them are familiar classics that, because of their beauty or historical significance, all but selected themselves. But most of the illustrations in these pages have been published rarely, if ever. The majority of the photographs were taken in black-and-white (although that term does not do justice to the luminescence of the best work of the Rosenfelds). The transition to color began in the early 1970's, when boating magazines began to publish more polychrome pictures. The medium is not the whole message: many of Stanley Rosenfeld's color pictures are distinguished by the same intriguing, complex shadings and compositions as the best of his and his father's black-and-white work. For instance, compare two photos of hard-charging big yachts taken from almost the same angle at an interval of 51 years: the photo of *Ranger* on page 57 with the one of *New Zealand* on pages 122-123. The eye never is bored.

Enough of words. Let's have a look at the pictures and the story they tell.

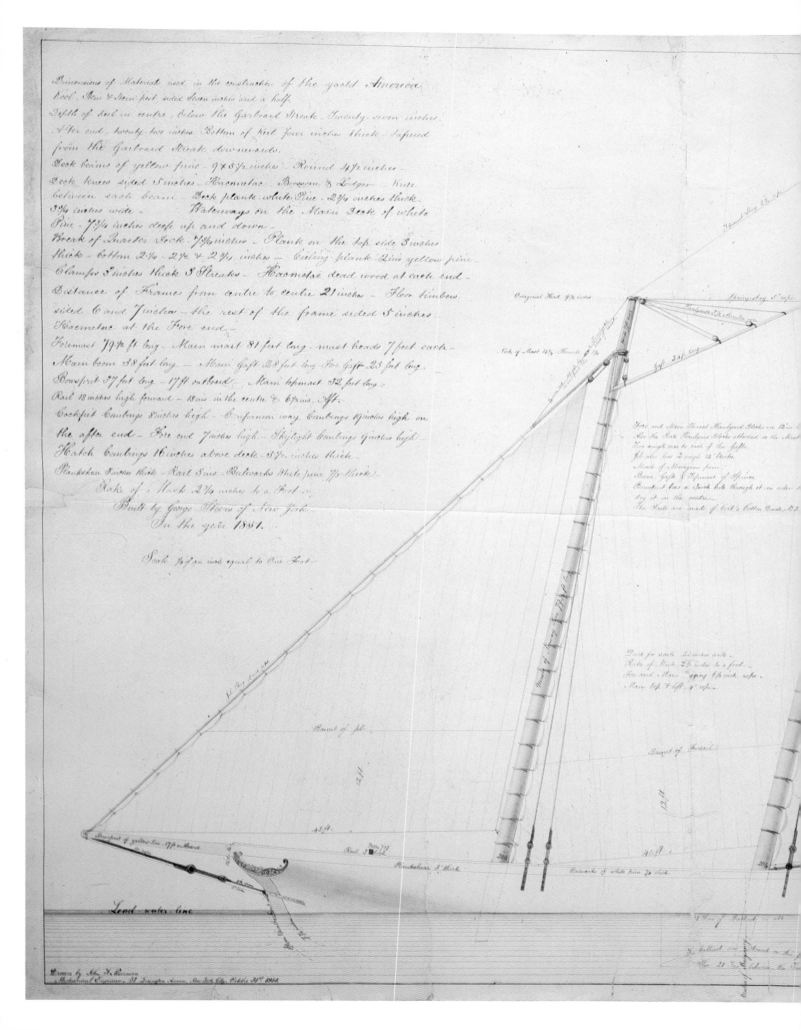

Dimensions of Materials used in the construction of the yacht America

Keel, Stem & Stern post sided Seven inches and a half.

Depth of keel in centre, below the Garboard Streak Twenty-seven inches.

After end, twenty-two inches. Bottom of Keel four inches thick - tapered from the Garboard Streak downwards.

Deck beams of yellow pine - 9 x 5½ inches. Round 4½ inches.

Deck knees sided 5 inches - Hacmatac Bosom & Ledger - Knee between each beam - Deck plank white Pine - 2¾ inches thick. 5¾ inches wide - Waterways on the Main Deck of white Pine - 7¾ inches deep up and down -

Break of Quarter Deck 7½ inches - Plank on the top side 3 inches thick - bottom 2¼ - 2½ & 2¾ inches - Ceiling plank 2 ins yellow pine.

Clamps 3 inches thick 3 Streaks - Hacmatac dead wood at each end -

Distance of Frames from centre to centre 21 inches - Floor timbers sided 6 and 7 inches - the rest of the frame sided 5 inches Hacmatac at the Fore end -

Foremast 79½ ft long - Main mast 81 feet long - mast heads 7 feet each -

Main boom 58 feet long - Main Gaff 28 feet long For Gaff 25 feet long.

Bowsprit 37 feet long - 17 ft outboard - Main topmast 32 feet long -

Rail 18 inches high forward - 18 ins in the centre & 6½ ins Aft.

Cockpit Combings 8 inches high - Companion way Combings 19 inches high on the after end - Fore end 7 inches high - Skylight Combings 9 inches high -

Hatch Combings 16 inches above deck - 3½ inches thick -

Plankshere 3 ins thick - Rail 3 ins - Bulworks White pine 7/8 thick -

Rake of Mast 2¾ inches to a Foot -

Built by George Steers of New York.

In the year 1851.

Scale ⅜ of an inch equal to One Foot -

In 1851 Prince Albert, consort to Queen Victoria, sponsored a world's fair whose main purpose was to introduce foreign agricultural implements to British farmers. Manufacturers in the United States, a new nation then considered something of an industrial backwater, sent over samples of many products besides plows and hoes. Among them was a schooner-rigged yacht, patriotically named *America*. Her New York Yacht Club syndicate of gambler sportsmen hoped she would win some one-on-one challenge matches against British yachts (and the hefty wagers that would accompany those matches). In the end, British farmers acquired some new tools, American manufacturers gained international respect, and on August 22, 1851, *America* won a race and a trophy that has since been raced for 27 times in one and one-half centuries.

America's steeply raked masts and sharp concave bow, clearly shown on this plan drawn in October 1851, startled her British hosts. "If she's right," said one yachtsman, "then we're all wrong." Still, she wasn't much different from the New York pilot boats designed by her architect, George Steers.

The small steep-roofed building in the left center was the first summer club-house of the New York Yacht Club after its founding in 1844. It was located on the Hudson River in New Jersey, on property belonging to the Stevens family of prominent yachtsmen. The building now is an exhibit at Mystic Seaport.

The founding Commodore, the sharp-eyed John Cox Stevens (1785-1857), was a legendary sportsman who won and lost thousands of dollars on horse and yacht races. He headed *America*'s six-man syndicate.

Thanks to her owners' well-publicized ambitions, *America* attracted lots of attention. Showing her under construction, this engraving appeared in the *Illustrated London News*. About 100 feet long on deck, she cost $20,000.

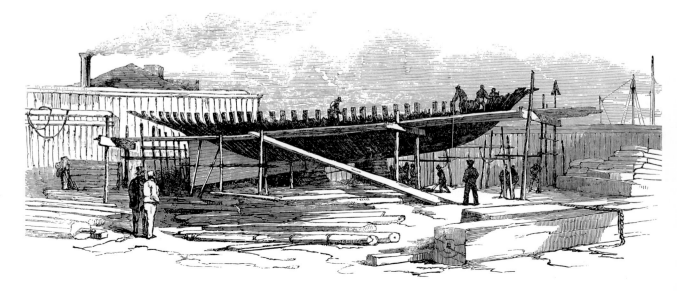

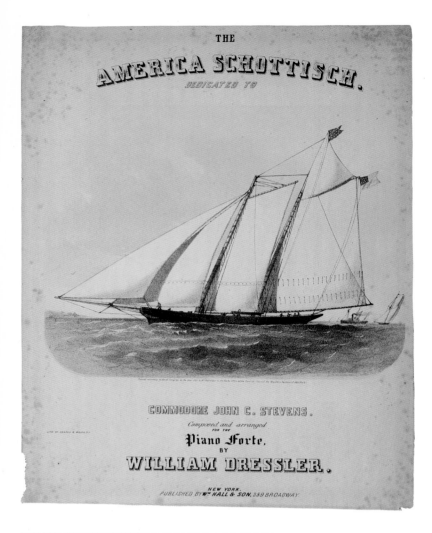

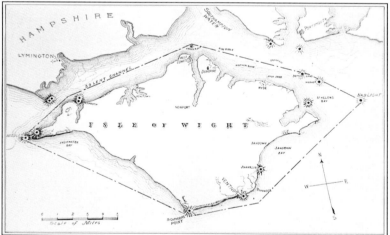

(Top) This sheet music cover was just one sign of the instant celebrity acquired by the schooner and her owners. Stevens and his partners became national heroes for insecure Americans who hungered for world recognition.

(Above) Once *America* showed off her speed, prominent English yachtsmen ignored Stevens' challenges. He was left with second-best: the Royal Yacht Squadron race around the Isle of Wight for "yachts belonging to the clubs of all nations." *America* easily won over 13 of the Squadron's schooners and cutters.

With her low black hull and stark rig, *America* was called "piratical." Many yachts soon were rebuilt along her radical lines. She sailed in European waters for several years, had a colorful career during the American Civil War, and eventually became a training vessel at the U.S. Naval Academy.

(Left) America's victory in the Squadron Cup race caused an international sensation. The United States suddenly was regarded as a new maritime power that had taught the master a lesson.

A few days after the Squadron Cup race, the syndicate unsentimentally sold *America* at a profit and returned to New York in triumph. Stevens gave this handsome cup as a token of thanks to one of the carpenters who built her.

Big racing schooners in the New York Yacht Club fleet swing from their anchors off Newport, Rhode Island, in 1872. According to one visiting yachtsman, this sleepy commercial port was "a tolerably dull place of sojournment." Newport later became a playground for the rich and a yachting center. After the America's Cup race course was moved from New York in 1930, Newport hosted 12 Cup matches through 1983.

The *America* syndicate presented the trophy to the New York Yacht Club. According to its Deed of Gift it was to be "perpetually a Challenge Cup for friendly competition between foreign countries." To make sure challengers would not have to endure the disappointments they had experienced in 1851, the syndicate established conditions that required a race even if the two sides could not agree on conditions. (The Deed was rewritten in 1882 and 1887 to take new problems into account.) The first challenger, in 1870, was James Ashbury. He got into a dispute over the meaning of the word "match," the word used in the Deed to describe the race. Ashbury said it required a one-on-one contest, but the New York Yacht Club sent out its entire fleet of schooners against his *Cambria*, which finished tenth out of 17 entrants. So much for "friendly competition." Not until the 1988 dispute between Michael Fay and the San Diego Yacht Club over the use of a catamaran defender would there be another major falling-out over fundamental rules. Ashbury came back in 1871 and got most of what he asked for. His *Livonia* won a race but lost the series, 4-1. Not until the 13th match in 1920 would a challenger win another race; not until the 25th match in 1983 would a challenger win the Cup. Against such odds, it seems strange that anybody challenged at all. What drew challengers back was a combination of some close racing, the Cup's glamour, and hope.

(Above) *Cambria*'s sturdy helmsmen do their job while the crew dodges spray. Note the variety of headgear. Not until the 1880's was the Cup covered by photographers.

(Right) Under sails made unbelievably voluptuous by artistic license, *Magic* leads the fleet home from the outer mark in the 1870 race as *Cambria* (second from left) slogs to windward.

(Left above) Like most racing boats of her day, the first Cup defender, *Magic*, wasn't much more than a refined fishing schooner.

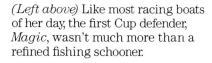

(Left below) An honored (but rotting) national relic, *America* lies at Annapolis, Maryland, in 1940. The official points out her still-elegant scrollwork. She was broken up in 1945 in her 95th year.

(Right) Taken on board *America* when she was owned by politician Benjamin Butler between 1874 and 1893, these early sailing photographs hint at what she was like on her great day in 1851.

Titled "A Stern Chase is a Long Chase," this lovely painting by Frederic S. Cozzens shows the defender *Madeleine* leading the Canadian *Countess of Dufferin* in the third match, in 1876. Tagging along as an unofficial contestant is the 25-year-old *America*, which soon passed the challenger. Prints made from Cozzens paintings are still found in yacht clubs.

Crowded by spectator steamers, Ashbury's *Livonia* trails *Sappho* in 1871. The New York Yacht Club sent out one defender each day, but reserved the right to use different yachts. *Sappho* won two races; *Columbia* won two races but lost one.

Cozzens shows the 1881 defender *Mischief* almost
leaping into our laps as she runs away from the Canadian *Atalanta*, whose spinnaker pole seems to be
bending to the breaking point. These sloops were only
about 70 feet long, some 30 feet shorter than the schooners of the first three matches. Most early races were
held in the narrow channels of New York Bay.

Amazingly, this is the interior of an America's Cup
yacht. *Galatea* came over in 1886 with piles of Turkish
rugs, a pack of dogs, and a pet monkey named Peggy,
who ran around in a sailor's uniform and hauled on
lines. Unfortunately, idiosyncratic charm counts for
nothing on the race course. This floating Victorian
drawing room was beaten badly by the less beguiling
but much faster *Mayflower*, the second of three Edward
Burgess-designed defenders that came from Boston,
Massachusetts.

(Top) Puritan, the 1885 winner over *Genesta*, makes knots. The Cup yachts of this period were about 100 feet long on deck and 85 feet long on the waterline.

(Above) The plumb-bowed, gaff-rigged contenders of the 1880's had a grace not found in any of the other generations of yachts that have sailed for the Cup. They seem to meld with the water.

(Left) Trained as an entomologist, the scholarly Edward Burgess (1848-1891) carried a scientific approach into his short but very successful career as a yacht designer. His last Cup boat was the 1887 defender, *Volunteer.*

Professional racing sailors like these fellows on *Puritan* were a rough-and-ready crowd. An entire crew might be recruited from a fishing village in the spring, race through the summer, and return home to tend lines all winter. Like many of the illustrations on pages 16-20, this is from a collection of lantern slides that was given to Mystic Seaport in 1986.

(*Top*) Their life had its dramas. At the start of a race in 1885, *Puritan* was caught on port tack by *Genesta* and suffered a pierced mainsail for her pains. She was immediately disqualified. *Genesta* withdrew rather than accept a hollow victory.

(*Above*) When a bowsprit wasn't attacking, it was a slippery platform for soaked deckhands working under the inflexible command of the mate.

"It is a game for the wealthy," said the yacht designer Nathanael Herreshoff of the America's Cup, "so let them choose the type and size of craft." In the ten years from the eighth match in 1893 through the 12th match in 1903, the wealthy owners – Morgans, Vanderbilts, Thomas Lipton, and others – chose to spend increasingly large sums of money on increasingly cutaway hulls that careened around under towering, fragile rigs. More money, higher ambitions, and the design genius of Nat Herreshoff and other naval architects produced these giants, which the British called "the Big Class." About 90 feet in waterline length and more than 120 from bow to stern, they flew as much as 17,000 square feet of canvas. In sheer forcefulness, these monsters never have been equalled.

(Below) Pure potential: the two-time Cup defender *Columbia* snoozes on a still morning in the Herreshoff yard in Bristol, Rhode Island. When her mast is stepped and her gear is brought aboard, she'll settle another couple of feet into the water and be ready for action.

Genesta – Challenger 1885

Puritan – Defender 1885

Valkyrie II – Challenger 1893

Vigilant – Defender 1893

Shamrock – Challenger 1899

Columbia – Defender 1899

(*Above*) Pure action: *Constitution* thrusts ahead in full flight, the embodiment of power under sail.

(*Left*) This illustration from a contemporary magazine shows the progression in design from the chesty boats of 1885 (top row) to the slim machines of 1899 (bottom row).

(*Right*) Nat Herreshoff (1848-1938) designed and built every America's Cup defender from 1893 through 1920, and the yard he once ran built the 1930 and 1934 defenders – in all, that's eight matches and a third of America's Cup history.

The big yachts were complicated creatures demanding close coordination among all their human elements. The team that sailed a Cup yacht, said Nat's son L. Francis Herreshoff, had "one head or brain (the captain), several mouthpieces (the mates), and 20 or 50 bunches of sinew, muscle, and leather which acted instantly at each order." He might have added, "one bank (the owner) to pay the bills and one executive (the manager) to keep everything running smoothly." This great body concentrated its efforts on a season of just a few months and less than 20 races.

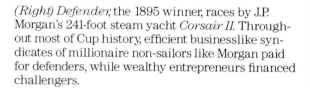

(Right) Defender, the 1895 winner, races by J.P. Morgan's 241-foot steam yacht *Corsair II.* Throughout most of Cup history, efficient businesslike syndicates of millionaire non-sailors like Morgan paid for defenders, while wealthy entrepreneurs financed challengers.

The best manager was C. Oliver Iselin (facing the camera), a banker and cutthroat racing sailor who ran four Cup winners. The man behind him holds a stadimeter, a device that measures distance and indicates who is gaining and dropping back.

The most colorful challenger-entrepreneur was the widely beloved, stylish Thomas Lipton (1850-1931), who challenged five times in 31 years, always in boats called *Shamrock,* and always without winning.

Captain Charlie Barr won three straight Cup matches. He was as cold-blooded as his bosses. It was once said of his behavior in a race, "Barr violated all rules of civilized warfare." His salary, $2500, was the price of a mainsail.

(Left) Charlie Barr's command was total. Reported *The Rudder* magazine, "About him for a space of ten feet the deck was absolutely clear, except just in front sat one man who never moved, and kept his eyes in front." Here he leans into the helm of the 1903 defender *Reliance* as his 63-man crew stays out of his way.

(Left) Simply setting sail on these great vessels was a major logistical problem. Under the supervision of the dark-suited mates, who guide the gaff with lines, *Reliance*'s huge crew sweats the mainsail aloft. Note the size of her mast.

(Right) Once the mainsail is set, it's time for the great topsail. Topmastmen balancing on the spreaders and gaff feed *Reliance*'s enormous topsail aloft as dozens of their shipmates haul on the halyards.

The photographs on these two pages are from scrapbooks of the 1895 campaign in *Defender* and the 1899 campaign in *Columbia.* The scrapbooks were kept and given to Mystic Seaport by Mrs. C. Oliver Iselin, who sailed aboard several defenders managed by her husband. Above, daredevils work out on *Columbia*'s long boom. The blurred water indicates how fast she was going. Occasionally, sailors (few of whom could swim) were lost from speeding Cup boats.

(Left) As her deckhands scramble to their positions, one of *Columbia*'s mates casts a worried look aloft. Just ahead is a competitor. Like the other boats that sailed against *Columbia* in 1899, she didn't stay ahead for long. *Columbia* came back to defend again in 1901.

(Right) Nat Herreshoff tenses as *Defender* rounds a mark boat (under the flag over his shoulder). The photographer has focused on the other yacht. Herreshoff sailed in the big Cup yachts he produced and occasionally got into disputes with Oliver Iselin and the captains about equipment and tactics.

(Left) Defender's debonair amateur afterguard shares a private joke as they overlook white-bearded, tight-lipped Captain Hank Haff. The middle gentleman's glance seems to ask, "Why don't you follow our advice, you old shellback?" Staring off, the captain thinks, "Why won't you busybodies leave me alone?" Haff sailed on four Cup winners between 1881 and 1895; he commanded two of them.

(Right) The races often were very close. A mate clears a line as *Columbia* barely leads *Shamrock* at the end of the first leg in the third race of the 1899 match. In a 20-knot breeze, *Columbia* (averaging 11 knots) has slowly overhauled *Shamrock* to take a narrow 17-second lead at the mark. One journalist called it "the finest 15-mile run in international yachting history."

The spinnaker was the sky-filling element in the Big Class's "cloud of sail." In 1899, *Columbia*'s crew muscles the tree-trunk-sized pole outboard while the stopped spinnaker, already hoisted, hangs in the vacuum of the mainsail's lee. Next the sail will be hauled out to the end of the pole on a traveler and opened with a strain on the sheet. Astern, three men aloft guide *Shamrock*'s spinnaker up.

With a mate on her bowsprit searching through binoculars for the next mark, *Columbia* (foreground) runs bow to bow with *Constitution* in 1901. Though older and slower, *Columbia* had one big advantage: her skipper was Charlie Barr, whom the yachting journalist W.P. Stephens once described as "handling *Columbia* as a man would a bicycle." An underdog all summer, the 1899 defender beat *Constitution* in the elimination trials and then scraped by *Shamrock II* in the Cup races.

There are times when even a spinnaker the size of a small castle can't do much to help. This is *Reliance* in misery.

Give it some wind and a big spinnaker is a photographer's dream, albeit a crew's nightmare. As *Defender* barrels along at maximum speed, passing a fleet of luxury yachts and a small boat (under her bowsprit), a dozen men yank on the spinnaker's foot to shake the wind out of the sail so they can corral it on deck. Already set for windward work are the jib and forestaysail. Before the 1930's, spinnakers were set with the sheet to windward of the headstay.

Taken earlier on the same leg, when *Defender* was racing along
under big reaching jib and spinnaker, this closeup suggests the
extent of the foredeck gang's predicament. Lying over the bow
is the stopped jib, which soon will be hoisted as it is hanked
onto the headstay.

Reliance rockets downwind with all 17,000 square feet pulling. Notice the bend in the 84-foot-long spinnaker pole. In order to get these boats in a full frame, the photographer had to back off until the crews looked like ants.

After catching *Shamrock* on the windy run in the
last race in 1899 (see page 27), *Columbia* crosses
the finish line at the Sandy Hook lightship under
reduced rig. Nobody liked to take the delicate Big
Class yachts out in strong winds, but sometimes
they were caught out by a squall and had to be
nursed along to avoid damage.

Constitution's crew secures her shattered gaff. The boats were most fragile aloft, where strength was sacrificed to light weight in order to reduce heeling force. *Constitution* lost in 1901 partly because she could not stay in one piece.

Reliance's light, retracting topmast collapses and takes the headstay and jib with it. This was her only big embarrassment during her triumphant summer of 1903.

Splendid luck is not the least important attribute of a good sailing photographer. James Burton was in the right place and looking in the right direction when the topsail, topmast, and bowsprit simultaneously parted company with *Vigilant,* the 1893 defender.

America's Cup racing almost died in 1895 when the challenger, the Earl of Dunraven, accused the Americans of cheating. Though the charges were proved groundless, in their backwash no British yachtsman from the Royal Yacht Squadron would challenge for the Cup. And then there appeared the driven but genial Thomas Lipton. No doubt motivated in part by a passion for publicity that would help his international food and tea empire, Lipton also loved the give and take of one-on-one challenges. He was the quintessential Cup challenger: an entrepreneur who had earned his fortune the hard way and now wanted to make his mark at the top level of the international sporting world. Lipton's amiability and sportsmanship – plus some thrilling racing – soon made everybody forget the animosities of the Dunraven incident.

(Left) His boom swinging daringly close to *Shamrock II*'s rigging, Charlie Barr in *Columbia* drives over the challenger before a start in 1901. The yachting journalist Winfield M. Thompson described this hard-fought match in these quaint words: "The great racing machines were tacked, jibed, and put about as easily as small raters, approaching each other within biscuit-toss." The winning margins averaged less than 2 minutes.

It helped that the boats and crews were becoming increasing accessible to the public thanks to more handy cameras. During a day on board *Reliance,* James Burton showed what it was like to sail the big yachts. What stands out in these close-ups of *Reliance*'s crew muzzling the spinnaker and mainsail are the teamwork of the beefy professional crews and the lively contrast between them and the gentlemen who paid their salaries.

In one of the low points in the history of the America's Cup, in 1895 *Defender* (right) limps along under her kinked rig at the start of the second race. William Cranfield tried to sail the Earl of Dunraven's *Valkyrie III* over *Defender* but – no Charlie Barr – he got too close and his boom took out her topmast shroud and her topmast bent almost double. *Valkyrie* won the race but was disqualified. The unrepentant Dunraven refused to sail the next race and later accused the Americans of cheating.

In one of the high points in Cup history, at the end of what a newspaper called "a Homeric contest" in 1901, *Shamrock II* (left) and *Columbia* luff across the finish line in a near dead heat. *Shamrock* split the line 2 seconds before *Columbia* but lost the race on handicap by 41 seconds. Not until 1962 would there be a closer victory.

Vigilant and *Valkyrie II* start a race in Dunraven's first, happier challenge in 1893. Big spectator fleets were such a problem that the crews of the Cup contenders hung "Keep Away!" signs in the rigging. Estimates of crowd size ran as high as 30,000 people.

The era of the Big Class ended with the unbeaten *Reliance*, the ultimate product of the imagination, money, and skill of Nat Herreshoff, Oliver Iselin, and Charlie Barr. Here she pulls away from *Shamrock III* as spectator steamers struggle to keep up.

Although contemporaries disparaged her looks – Thomas Fleming Day of *The Rudder* called her "an overgrown, ugly brute" – at certain angles *Reliance* showed a touch of grace.

The largest single-masted sailboat ever built
stretches over the ways. The perfectionist Oliver
Iselin never took her for granted. The greatest praise
he offered her in his log was, "On the whole the
performance of the *Reliance* is most satisfactory."
When he wrote that, she had just whipped
Shamrock in the first Cup race by more than 7 minutes. By winter 1904 *Reliance* was a heap of scrap
metal. The rest of the Big Class followed soon after.

The large model room is a museum of the history of yacht design. Hung on the walls are hundreds of half-models of ships and pleasure boats, and displayed in cases are full-rigged models of *America* (in the center of the room) and all yachts that raced for her Cup before 1988.

On the building's exterior, the area of the bay windows was designed to look like the stern of a great Renaissance sailing ship. This is one of the most startling sights on the streets of New York.

By the 1890's, the New York Yacht Club and America's Cup racing were symbols of vast wealth and prestige for industrialists and financiers in the generation of J.P. Morgan. But while there was a modest clubhouse in New York City and waterfront stations in several harbors, none of the New York Yacht Club's facilities fully reflected its grandeur. In 1898, Morgan gave the club a plot of valuable land on Manhattan's 44th Street for a new clubhouse. Designed by William Warren in a gaudy style called "eclectic," it could be called a temple to yachting. These pictures show it – main features not much changed – in the 1970's, when the America's Cup still was on display in a small trophy room inside. In all, the New York Yacht Club held the Cup for 132 years, from 1851 to 1983, and successfully defended it 24 consecutive times. Counting the 1983 match, when the Cup finally was wrested away by Alan Bond's *Australia II*, the club's defending yachts won 84 races and lost only 12. Not only was this winning streak the longest in sporting history, it was the most dominant.

(Top) America memorabilia surround the main staircase (here decorated for Christmas). Hanging on the lobby wall are her original tiller and carved-wood transom eagle, which was found in an English pub and presented to the club by the Royal Yacht Squadron. In the stairwell to the left is a handsome primitive painting of the yacht winning the Cup.

(Above) The decorations around the bay windows were designed to resemble the first pleasure boats as they evolved in the Netherlands in the 17th century. These little vessels were called *jacht schips,* "swift boats." "*Jacht*" eventually evolved into "yacht."

The elegant gentlemen in *Shamrock IV's* afterguard may
look like they belong on the sidelines of a cricket match,
but before 1983 no other challengers came closer to winning. Luck was in their favor: they won the first race after
Resolute broke down and the second after a big wind
shift. All they had to do was win one of the next three
races. They didn't.

When the 13th match was held in 1920 (after being postponed since 1914 by World War I), the boats were about two-thirds the size of *Reliance* and her cousins. This was the first Cup match between amateur skippers. Charles Francis Adams (a descendant of two U.S. Presidents) commanded the defending *Resolute* and William P. Burton was at the helm of *Shamrock IV.* This also was the first Cup match covered by Morris Rosenfeld. Almost all the photographs in this book up to here were taken by James Burton and Charles Edwin Bolles (whose collections Rosenfeld purchased in 1910).

Resolute (between a ferry boat and J.P. Morgan Jr.'s *Corsair III*) almost disappears behind a cloud of black smoke spread by the usual mob of spectator steamers.

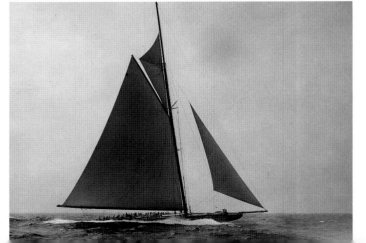

Shamrock IV surfs wildly in 30 knots of wind before the start of the fifth race, which soon will be postponed until the next day. *Resolute* won the race and the match, 3-2. This *Shamrock* was ugly. Alfred F. Loomis described her as "something like a cross between a tortoise and an armored cruiser."

Resolute (white) and Shamrock inch away from the starting line in the fog and light wind that haunted most of the 1920 match. This was the last of the 13 matches sailed off New York. Looking for more wind and smaller spectator fleets, the New York Yacht Club moved the races to Newport. This also was the last match sailed by boats carrying the broad, symmetrical gaff rig.

The William Gardner-designed Vanitie was the most beautiful of the new boats, but (alas) Resolute beat her in the defenders' eliminations. This photograph, one of the Rosenfelds' most famous, is the epitome of the majestic style of yachting illustration. When the delicate shadings and artistic compositions of first-rate black-and-white photography are enhanced by subtle darkroom work, who needs color?

The time when "Tommy" Lipton returned every couple of years was long past. The 1930 match (only the fourth since 1900 and Lipton's last) introduced the modern era in the America's Cup, with a new venue at Newport and a new incarnation of the Big Class in the efficient, Marconi-rigged sloops that fit into the "J" class of the Universal Rule. These great sloops ranged in overall length from 120 to 135 feet and in waterline length from 80 to 87 feet. The era first was dominated by Harold S. Vanderbilt (1884-1970), the only skipper besides Charlie Barr to take the Cup three times running. Unlike Barr, he was a millionaire amateur skipper who owned part or all of his Cup defenders. This gifted man won easily in 1930, barely escaped disaster in 1934, and then, after taking pains to make sure his next boat was unbeatable, completely dominated in 1937.

Behind Vanderbilt's boyish grin lay the ruthless competitiveness and passion for efficiency of an Oliver Iselin and a Charlie Barr. Yet Vanderbilt was not inhuman. After shattering Lipton's last hopes, he sympathetically wrote in *Enterprise's* log, "Our hour of triumph, our hour of victory, is all but at hand, but it is so tempered with sadness that it is almost hollow."

In *Enterprise,* victor over *Shamrock V,* Vanderbilt had the pure racing machine. Here is her stripped-out interior looking forward toward the mast, which was held together by 80,000 rivets and built of a high-tech aluminum alloy called duralumin. Many of her sailors worked down here on winches originally used in *Reliance.* Later, the rules were changed to require accommodations for the professional crew.

One of the innovations of *Enterprise's* designer,
W. Starling Burgess, an aircraft pioneer, was the wide
"Park Avenue" boom that allowed the mainsail's foot
to slide from side to side to assume the best shape.
Working at an interval of 50 years, Starling and his
father, Edward, designed a total of six defenders.

(Left) *Enterprise* finishes a race near one of the tugs carrying photographers and reporters. Harold Vanderbilt was as aggressive at the helm as he was courageous in supporting new technology. In the days before low-stretch, high-strength sail fabrics, three small cotton jibs held their shape better than one or two big ones. Vanderbilt would go on to use the first synthetic sail ever built in *Ranger* in 1937.

Vanderbilt's carefully organized Cup campaigns included small fleets of support craft. Here *Enterprise* is shepherded closely by his big power-boat *Vara,* in which he and his afterguard slept and ate.

Vanderbilt (wearing the visor) leaves his 1937 defender *Ranger* in a small launch. On *Ranger,* an elaborate bending boom with struts and adjustable stays replaced the Park Avenue boom. Because the Great Depression discouraged Cup syndicates, Vanderbilt personally covered *Ranger*'s cost, estimated at more than $500,000.

With a typically determined look on his face, Thomas Sopwith (1888-1989), the owner and skipper of the 1934 and 1937 challengers, poses for the camera with his jauntily dressed wife, Phyllis, who served in his afterguard (as Gertrude Vanderbilt did in *Ranger*). A pioneer aviator – "We had a lot of crashes in those days," he once recalled, "but, bless you, it was fun" – Sopwith had the right mix of daring and technical skill, but he was not Vanderbilt's match as a manager.

Another *Corsair* (the third we have seen) stands by as *Endeavour*'s crew douses a jib after the finish of a race in 1934. Since *Endeavour* easily won the first two races, Commodore J.P. Morgan Jr. no doubt was a bit anxious. But Vanderbilt and *Rainbow* came back to win, 4-2.

(Right) Their stopped spin-nakers snaking aloft, *Endeavour* and *Rainbow* square off for a running start. They often sailed very close to each other, and there were several bitterly contro-versial claims of fouls.

(Far right) Endeavour's crew, who had every reason to expect to win, watches the spinnaker come down on *Rainbow* after the finish of the sixth and last race. The holes in *Endeavour*'s huge parachute spinnaker were a short-lived fad. Flying in her rigging is a protest flag concerning a perceived vio-lation of the racing rules; the protest never was heard.

After his scare in 1934, Vanderbilt took special pains to build a fast boat next time around. She was *Ranger,* which dominated the 1937 Cup season as thoroughly as *Reliance* had done in 1903. Here *Ranger* (left) thunders by *Rainbow* in a trial race. Both boats carry quadrilateral jibs, whose stretch is controlled by two sets of sheets.

(Left) In *Ranger*'s design team and afterguard were the young brothers Rod and Olin Stephens, here shown adjusting one of her enormous turnbuckles under the scrutiny of Vanderbilt (in the visor). According to Olin Stephens, Starling Burgess was chiefly responsible for *Ranger*'s design.

(Right) Rainbow leaves a river of foam in her wake as she slices toward Block Island. A typical J-Boat crew included 26 professionals and five amateurs in the afterguard.

(Above) Though more simple than the gaff-rigged Cup yachts of the past, the J's still were complex machines. This is *Endeavour*'s deck. The two sailors are snugging a halyard.

(Above right) *Ranger*'s crew bends on her 2000-pound mainsail. Vanderbilt had it taken off each evening to allow him complete freedom to choose whichever sail best fit the conditions the next day.

(Right) *Ranger*'s crew lived forward in a large cabin that included sail-handling equipment, including a chute used to feed jibs on deck. The photo is taken from an owner's cabin.

Hard on the wind in a moderate breeze with her snub bow lifting to a wave, *Ranger* charges along at full horsepower. She beat *Endeavour II* by an average of more than 11 minutes and won 32 of 34 races in the summer of 1937. *"Ranger,"* wrote Vanderbilt, "had a habit of doing almost everything you asked her to do."

(Left) Vanderbilt wrote of this photograph in his book *On the Wind's Highway:* "With out-stretched wings, white as snow, they are flying towards us in formation. *Ranger,* the fastest all-around sailing vessel that has ever been built, heads the caval-cade. Her four older sisters follow in her train. Soaring, a fresh breeze fills the world's largest sail."

(Right) Rainbow – now sailed in a fairly relaxed manner by the Hovey family – slides along in 1937. Owner Chandler Hovey stands between his son Buss (steering) and daughter Sis. Loung-ing on the main sheet are the mate and Captain Gus Olsen, who glances at the photographer. Sis Hovey remembers that none of the 22 Norwegian crew members could speak English "but fortu-nately we could understand Gus and the first mate." This is one of the most graceful photographs of a Cup boat.

Even on board *Ranger* there were times when competitive juices cooled. As Vanderbilt steers and Olin Stephens (standing) reflects on the day's events, Rod Stephens, balancing on a winch, squeezes out a tune.

Say farewell to *Enterprise* and the other J-Class yachts, which
became painfully expensive to build and sail. Most J's were
broken up (two exceptions were the first *Endeavour* and
Shamrock V, which still are sailing). When the 17th match
finally was held in 1958, the Cup contenders were yachts one-
half the size and one-third the cost of the J's.

The 12-Meter *Intrepid* swings into a jibe ahead of *Constellation* during a trial race in 1967. Though not as majestic and fast as the J's and Big Class, the 12-Meters were much more maneuverable. They provided competition whose breathtaking, regular keenness was unprecedented in Cup history. Their smaller size also meant that the sailors finally could star on camera.

With the end of the J's, the America's Cup seemed an anachronism. After much talk about alternatives, in 1956 the New York Yacht Club requested changes in the Deed of Gift from the Supreme Court of the State of New York, the Cup's guardian after the death of the members of *America*'s syndicate. These changes allowed the use of relatively modest boats that could be transported to Cup races on the decks of ships. The boat that the club had in mind was the 12-Meter, named for a category in the International Rule. About 65 feet long and with a crew of 11, Twelves were thought of as small boats in the heyday of the J Class, but they seemed to get bigger and bigger during every year of postwar economic inflation. The Royal Yacht Squadron opened the era of the 12-Meters by challenging for the Cup in 1958.

(Top) The framed-up hull of *Columbia* lies behind scaffolding. Ironically, the new boats brought traditional wooden boatbuilding back into the America's Cup, most of whose contenders since the 1880's were constructed of metal.

(Above) Craftsmen at the Nevins boatyard, on City Island, New York, shape *Columbia*'s deadwood with traditional adzes.

In the classic ceremony that will be repeated as long as people care for boats, the sponsor smashes a bottle of champagne on the new yacht's bow and names her *Columbia*.

Columbia's sponsor, Mary Sears, waits to perform the ritual. *Columbia* went on to be the third yacht of her name to defend the Cup. The first was a schooner in 1871, the second a Big-Class sloop that defended in both 1899 and 1901.

(Left) Columbia's "brain" at work: skipper Briggs Cunningham talks tactics with Olin Stephens while navigator Henry Sears looks on. Rarely in Cup history are key sailing roles played by the designer (here, Stephens) and the owner (Cunningham and Sears, members of Columbia's syndicate).

(Left) Meanwhile, there's still a need for muscle and agility. Rod Stephens goes aloft on the spinnaker pole to clear a halyard.

(Right) Columbia (in the distance) easily leads the challenger Sceptre, which is knocked over by her overly full sails. The British challenger proved uncompetitive as soon as the two boats sailed side-by-side.

(1) Just after the start *Weatherly* (US17) and *Gretel*, water rushing over their decks, charge off on port tack into the westerly wind and afternoon sun. Stanley Rosenfeld, following close behind, quickly takes advantage of the backlit action scene that was his and his father's favorite kind of photograph.

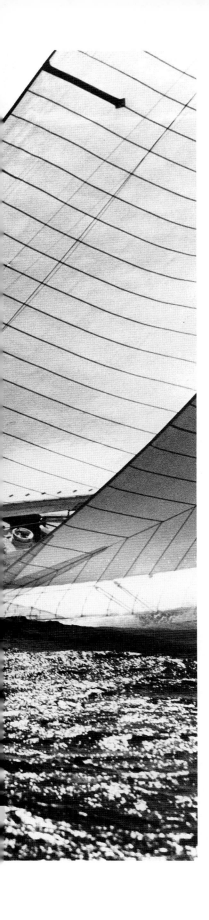

When the first Australian challenger, *Gretel*, arrived in Newport in 1962 there were hopes for a better match than the British had produced four years earlier. Hope was transformed into anticipation when *Gretel* showed speed while losing the first race. In the second race, anticipation became reality. In 20 knots of wind, Bus Mosbacher and *Weatherly* took a slight lead. Australian Jock Sturrock began to attack, and from then on the two boats were locked in a duel that is extraordinary not only because it was so thrilling but because it was thoroughly documented by Stanley Rosenfeld, the only photographer granted access to the inside of the course.

(2) The two boats drive on, bow to bow, slicing into the short chop.

(3) Sturrock tries to evade Mosbacher's wind shadow by tacking again and again. As the crews' arms flail, *Gretel*'s more powerful winches sheet in her big genoa jib a moment faster than *Weatherly*'s, and the Aussies gain foot by foot.

(4) After 8 miles of beating into it, the two boats round the first mark separated by only 12 seconds – one length of a boat. Sturrock's deckhands fling themselves onto the windward rail to lever *Gretel* upright another couple of degrees and speed her after *Weatherly*.

(5 and 6) They half-submarine down the reaching leg and, as the crews scramble to set the spinnakers, jibe around the tug that marks the turn for the finish.

(7, next page) A big wave out of the Atlantic crests under *Gretel* and gives her a thunderous ride. As her bulging spinnaker pulls her bow toward the stars, a euphoric sailor near her mast leans back and lets loose with a war whoop.

(8) More waves follow. Plowing a great furrow of white water, she careens along at twice the speed of poor *Weatherly,* which wallows in a patch of water so flat that one of her crew can stand on the afterdeck.

(9) Her momentum drives *Gretel*'s sharp bow through the face of the wave. *Weatherly*'s lead has all but disappeared.

(10) This is *Gretel*'s day. Another great wave lifts her, and she breaks ahead and is gone. The Aussies win by 47 seconds.

(11) The Americans lower their fractured spinnaker pole, broken as they tried to catch *Gretel*. This was *Gretel*'s only victory in 1962, but her fine performance in light wind in the fourth race (which she lost by only 26 seconds, the closest finish since 1901) made it clear that the New York Yacht Club had better be prepared when Australians next visited Newport.

Excitement in an America's Cup can take several forms – thrills at a tightly-fought race, awe at enormous yachts, sympathetic rooting for an underdog, or (as shown on the next six pages) amazement at the spectacle of talented people making a botch of things. As we have already seen in the breakdowns of the Big-Class boats (page 35), the America's Cup is no stranger to Murphy's Law ("What can go wrong *will* go wrong"). The issue is not whether Murphy comes aboard (he will), but whether he comes aboard when a photographer is nearby. Unfortunately for *Constellation* and *Gretel II,* Stanley Rosenfeld was in the neighborhood when Murphy paid his visits in 1964 and 1970.

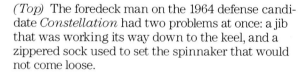

(Top) The foredeck man on the 1964 defense candidate *Constellation* had two problems at once: a jib that was working its way down to the keel, and a zippered sock used to set the spinnaker that would not come loose.

(Above) Now her entire crew has a chance to participate as they fish a spinnaker out of the briny. The look on the face of skipper Eric Ridder (right) speaks volumes.

(Left) After a dismasting, *Constellation*'s crew tries to keep everything on deck as they await a tow to port, where a replacement mast awaits them.

Constellation's gaffes did not go unnoticed by these gentlemen, the New York Yacht Club's America's Cup Committee. Seen here keeping a sharp eye on a race, they selected the defender based not just on the won-lost record but also on the reliability of crew and equipment. Their observation boat, *Djinn,* was the latest Morgan-owned yacht at Cup races (see pages 22, 45, and 53). J.P. Morgan's grandson Henry stands at the left.

Having survived the summer's gauntlet, *Constellation*'s crew celebrates winning the Cup with champagne smuggled aboard.

Constellation's temporary embarrassments were nothing compared with the walloping that she gave the British challenger, *Sovereign* (foreground). With the average winning margin greater than 12 minutes, this was one of the worst drubbings in Cup history.

Why all the headscratching? What are these men so worried about? Quite a lot, as it turns out. The crew of the 1970 Australian challenger *Gretel II* might have won the Cup had they not made a series of mistakes both big and small.

Gretel II (right) , close behind *Intrepid* at a turning mark, was a very fast boat when things went well, but not when her spinnaker pole was dragging in the water.

A *Gretel II* crewmember fell overboard in the first race against *Intrepid.* After picking him up, the Australians lost by almost 6 minutes. The next day, a newspaper article about the race was headlined, "Bad Dream at Newport."

In the second race, Bill Ficker in *Intrepid* (US22) aimed for a gap on the starting line between *Gretel II* and the race committee boat. *Gretel,* her jib luffing, headed up to close the gap and collided with *Intrepid.* Though left dead in the water, the very fast *Gretel* went on to overtake *Intrepid.* Later the Australians were disqualified by the race committee on the grounds that the rules prohibited their tactic once the start was signaled by the dark cylinder.

New York Yacht Club race committee chairman Devereux Barker somberly reads the decision to the press, which quickly fanned the matter into an international furor. *Intrepid,* sailed brilliantly by Ficker and his crew, ended up winning the match 4-1. She might well have lost had *Gretel II* been sailed as well as she deserved.

Intrepid had it a lot easier in 1967. Her designer was Olin Stephens (top row, right), her skipper was Bus Mosbacher (at the wheel), and her syndicate head was Bill Strawbridge (to Mosbacher's right). Her crew was composed wholly of amateurs.

Before an audience of official vessels, *Intrepid* drives over *Dame Pattie* at a start. This was as close as the Australians got to beating her in 1967. *Intrepid*'s domination was reminiscent of *Reliance* and *Ranger.*

(Right) In 1967, *Intrepid* nods to an Atlantic roller under the close supervision of her tender, which flies a syndicate flag. Olin Stephens took a hand in designing every Cup defender but one from *Ranger* in 1937 through *Courageous* in 1977. That's a total of seven matches in 40 years. The only exception was the Philip Rhodes-designed *Weatherly* in 1962.

Intrepid brought a whole new look to 12-Meters. This is before 1967: as *Constellation* crashes into a wave after a tack, helmsman Bob Bavier (in the white hat) peers around a wall of burly winch-grinders sheeting the genoa jib home. Bavier replaced Eric Ridder as helmsman in midsummer 1964 and guided *Constellation* to her Cup victory.

Olin Stephens (right, with skipper Bob McCullough) studies a model for *Valiant* in the towing tank at Stevens Institute (founded by John Cox Stevens' brother Edwin). While scientific research became increasingly important, it was not always constructive: *Valiant* was a loser in 1970.

To help crews measure performance precisely as well as navigate around the race course, sophisticated electronics and, later, compact computers were installed in Cup contenders. This is the navigator's station in the 1974 Cup defense candidate *Mariner*, an early aluminum Twelve.

Though the yachts were smaller and increasingly dependent on technology, manual labor and seamanship continued to play a major role in America's Cup sailing. As *Constellation* pounds through heavy weather, Rod Stephens shows concern about her mast. He had reason to worry: this picture was snapped a few minutes before the one at the bottom of page 74.

On another windy day, *Constellation* – her helmsman struggling for control – surges by an onlooking warship.

As *Valiant* works her way to windward during a tune-up sail, two crewmembers go aloft in bosun's chairs to adjust her rigging. For every hour a Cup contender's crew spends racing, they devote at least another five hours to boat maintenance.

When they aren't racing or taking care of the boat, the sailors are practicing sail-handling. This is *Constellation*'s crew in a sail drill.

While *Mariner*'s winches are ground at the command of the sail-trimmer standing in the cockpit on the right, tactician Dennis Conner (hand on winch) and skipper Ted Turner concentrate on their opponent. *Mariner* was a failure, but both men survived. One or the other was in every Cup defender from 1974 through 1988.

Skipper/yacht designer/sailmaker Ted Hood checks for weed on the rudder of *Nefertiti*, which finished second behind *Weatherly* in the 1962 defense trials. Like other players in the America's Cup game, Hood could not stay away; he, too, would come back to win a Cup match.

Although most 12-Meter sailors were not paid, there were a few benefits. This is *Intrepid*'s crew at dinner in 1967, with skipper Bus Mosbacher at the head of the table.

Brute force serves tactics. The 1974 challenger, *Southern Cross* (KA4), slows to try to fall into the favored tailing position behind *Courageous*, but the Americans move too fast. In *Courageous*, Ted Hood was skipper and Dennis Conner, who had started the summer in *Mariner,* was tactician and starting helmsman.

The 1974 Cup season was noteworthy for three reasons. First, the seven-year-old wooden two-time defender *Intrepid* (US22) battled the new aluminum *Courageous* down to the wire in the closest defense eliminations in years.

(Right) Courageous was selected to defend on the last possible day. She then beat *Southern Cross.* Here they duel near the U.S. Coast Guard training vessel *Eagle.*

Second, the towing tank on which designers had depended for so long produced a dud in *Mariner,* with her squared-off after sections and tiny keel and rudder. The first Twelve with a separated keel and rudder had been *Intrepid,* and *Mariner,* said the tank, was an improved *Intrepid.*

The third significant event in 1974 was the appearance of a brash new challenger, 36-year-old Western Australian Alan Bond, owner of *Southern Cross.* Bond promised to be around for a long time.

For years, the America's Cup was followed closely only within the sailing community. The world at large seemed to think of it not as a sport but as a kind of rare, private ornament of the wealthy. But when colorful, publicity-conscious characters – preeminently Alan Bond and Ted Turner – arrived on the scene in the 1970's, the Cup regained some of the broad public attention it had lost after the death of Thomas Lipton in 1931. The world also noticed and liked the fact that Cup racing was becoming even more international, with challengers in 1977 from Australia, France, and Sweden.

(Top) Like the early Cup races off New York City, the matches off Newport attracted tens of thousands of spectators – but they came out in their own small craft, not ferry boats.

(Above) Bob Bavier (in tie) moderates a crowded press conference in 1970 between *Gretel II*'s Jim Hardy (left) and *Intrepid*'s Bill Ficker. Cup yachtsmen now had to explain themselves to reporters who did not know one end of a boat from the other.

Nobody expected much from the boisterous television and sports executive Ted Turner (facing camera) when he was given command of *Courageous* in 1977. His boat, the 1974 winner, was three years old. His competitors, Ted Hood and Lowell North, were widely respected sailmakers with brand-new boats. And Turner's only previous Cup summer (with *Mariner* in 1974) had been a dismal failure. But Turner loved being the underdog as much as he took pleasure in meeting challenges.

Ted Turner, who sailed *Courageous* when she won again in 1977, gloried in head-to-head competition. Here he chases Hood's *Independence* in pre-start circling maneuvers during the summer's intense Cup-defense trials.

Turner, the last true amateur to win the America's Cup, takes a snooze. With a young college sailing coach named Gary Jobson as tactician, he surprised almost everybody by eliminating the professionals and then beating Alan Bond's *Australia*, 4-0.

While some men are attracted to the Cup for the sport it offers, others like its lifestyle. Here, in white gloves and uniform, is ballpoint pen manufacturer Baron Marcel Bich, the perennial French challenger from 1970 through 1980.

In *Courageous* in 1974, Ted Hood inspects a jib while skipper Bob Bavier looks on. Late that summer, the syndicate replaced Bavier with Hood, who went on to win the Cup. Ironically, Bavier had replaced Eric Ridder as helmsman of *Constellation* ten years earlier.

Here the syndicate chairman, the Aga Khan, cheers the Italian challenger *Azzurra* after she won a race in 1983. There were four challengers in 1980 and seven in 1983. After a long summer of elimination races, the eventual challenger was well prepared for the American defender.

Dennis Conner in *Freedom* leads *Australia* at a start in 1980. *Australia* gains sail area from her strange-looking hooked mast, an idea borrowed from the British challenger and later banned. She won one race and was always close. Conner was a master at starting a match race using aggressive tactics that go back to Charlie Barr and Harold Vanderbilt.

When Alan Bond was asked in 1980 why he had returned to Newport to challenge for the third time, he answered: "You go out there and you're as good as the next guy, who might be a Vanderbilt. You get out there and all you've got is a common element — the wind and the sea — and everybody's equal." That fascinating statement goes a long way toward explaining the personal ambitions of challengers. It also reflects the fact that Australian challengers had closed the technology gap to where they were consistently equal on the water. If challengers next could solve their chronic problem with bad organization, there was no reason why they should not take the Cup away within a few years. This did not go unnoticed in America. Dennis Conner, the winning tactician in 1974 and now a skipper, turned preparations for the 1980 match into a full-time job. His *Freedom* lost only four races in the defense eliminations and went on to beat Bond's *Australia* in a match a lot closer than the 4-1 results suggest. Anticipating an even tougher battle in 1983, Conner went into a full-scale program to gain a technological advantage. So, too, did Bond.

Conner's *Liberty* (the red boat) and Tom Black-aller's *Defender* circle tightly before a start in 1983, each skipper trying to position his bow close behind the other's stern. A close-tailing position is advantageous because, under the racing rules, the leading boat cannot make abrupt course changes that interfere with the tailing boat. This allows the tailing boat to push the leading boat away from the starting line, then turn back to start ahead.

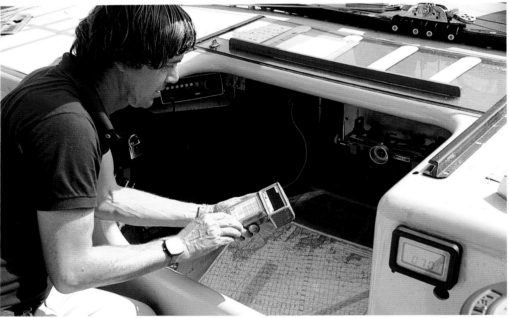

(Top) Bond's 1983 challenger *Australia II,* here tuning up off Newport, swept the 1983 challenge eliminations. She was designed by Ben Lexcen with the help of Dutch scientists. Her most radical feature, her keel, isn't visible here. In fact, the keel was kept from prying eyes until after the 1983 match against *Liberty.* Cup crews were brought back on deck by a rule change.

(Above) *Liberty* navigator Halsey Herreshoff (grandson of Nathanael Herreshoff) demonstrates an on-board hand-held computer terminal. By 1983, a 12-Meter's electronic instruments cost about as much as hull construction, and a syndicate's budget was approaching $6 million.

With an enormous flag dominating the Newport skyline, the Australian presence was becoming increasingly potent both off and on the water during Bond's fourth challenge in 1983.

If there was any place where the Aussie twang did not dominate, it was in the great Newport "cottages" like The Breakers (built by Harold Vanderbilt's uncle Cornelius in 1895). These massive summer homes had seen America's Cup challengers come and go without much effect. All that changed in 1983.

Finally unveiled after the 1983 match, here is *Australia II*'s secret keel. The wings improved the water flow and permitted a smaller hull with more sail area. All summer the keel's shape and legality were the subjects of bitter disputes that Alan Bond craftily played to his advantage.

Liberty and *Australia II* start the seventh race tied 3-3. Conner, knowing he has the slower boat, takes a chance on port tack to find better wind. The race was 24 miles long, and *Liberty* led for 20 of them. Unfortunately for Conner, they were the first 20 miles. *Australia II* won by 41 seconds.

(*Left*) Under code flags signaling, "Congratulations, Well Done," the New York Yacht Club race committee applauds *Australia II* and her crew after the last race. Other members of the club had tried their best all summer to get her disqualified. Americans were used to seeing challengers take the limelight, but nothing in Cup history matched the attention given *Australia II* and her mysterious keel.

As an exuberant Alan Bond holds it aloft, the America's Cup changes hands for the first time since the Royal Yacht Squadron presented it to John Cox Stevens in 1851. At the left is *Australia II* skipper John Bertrand, who like Bond had been trying for years to wrest the Cup from the New York Yacht Club.

Their exhausted faces showing the effects of a summer of acrimony and excruciating pressure, Conner, Bond, and Bertrand (with moderator Bill Ficker) answer questions at the press conference after the seventh race.

Maybe the America's Cup would be sailed for once again in the Atlantic Ocean, but for now it was off to distant waters. There remained memories of the great matches off Newport, like this one between *Courageous* and *Intrepid* in the glow of a late-afternoon calm in 1974.

When Cup racing resumed in October 1986, it was halfway around the world on the Indian Ocean off Fremantle, in Western Australia, under the aegis of Alan Bond's very capable Royal Perth Yacht Club. Five Australian boats battled it out for the right to defend, while 13 British, Canadian, French, Italian, and U.S. challenging yachts eliminated one another for the right to race against the Aussie defender. The arrival on the scene of the winged keel had brought temporary technological equality. In their efforts to optimize boats, keels, and sails, hopeful syndicates and owners poured millions of dollars into research. By one estimate, the 18 boats racing at Fremantle represented a total investment of more than $200 million. Unlike Newport, where light winds had prevailed, Fremantle provided fresh winds that tested crews and boats with a daily thrashing and (as a side benefit) turned the event into a fascinating spectator contest for people watching on television around the world. Sailors and onlookers alike were rewarded with competition that according to Stanley Rosenfeld was the best he had ever seen in 60 years of taking pictures of sailboat races.

This duel typifies the racing off Fremantle. During the challenger eliminations, *New Zealand* (left) rounded a buoy (ball on right) a few feet ahead of the New York Yacht Club's *America II.* Stanley Rosenfeld was there to record the ensuing tacking duel (next pages).

(Left) After turning the buoy (note the wakes), John Kolius in *America II* (right) came about onto starboard tack. Chris Dickson in *New Zealand* has followed in order to cover and stay between Kolius and the wind. But now Kolius pauses in midtack and goes back. (*Below*) Dickson again follows. (*Previous page*) His sheets may be tangled and his genoa jib may not be pulling, but Dickson is where he wants to be: directly upwind of *America II.*

(Top) Although both boats are almost stopped after all their violent maneuvers, Kolius tries yet again to get free. He swings *America II* around onto starboard tack. It's his third tack in less than a minute. (Below) This time he breaks free as Dickson stays on port tack in order to build up speed. Kolius has lost a lot of distance, but he has gained clear wind and, at least for the moment, is the master of his own destiny. *America II* finished fifth in the challenge elimination trials; the New York Yacht Club was out of the Cup for the first time.

New Zealand (right) and Dennis Conner in *Stars & Stripes* approach the starting line in one of the final elimination-series races to see who would sail against the Australians. The man on *New Zealand*'s bow gauges the distance to the starting line and the other boat and signals to Dickson.

Worldwide television coverage kept the air over the race course full of helicopters carrying camera crews and (here) ferrying videotape back to the studio ashore. Cameras on board the competing boats brought the excitement of competition directly into viewers' living rooms.

(Top) Crowds of well-wishers give a send-off to *Stars & Stripes* and her tune-up boat as they leave their docks for a race. The aggressive underdog Dennis Conner was a hero to Australians, who saw him as one of their own kind.

(Above) A fleet of megayachts follows one of the Cup races. All that was missing was J.P. Morgan in *Corsair*. Ironically, a much better view was had by people watching the races at home on their television sets.

(*Left*) Those spindly-legged beings from outer space are actually the shadows of foredeck crews setting up spinnaker gear on the nearly over-lapped *Eagle* and *Italia*.

At a typically close mark-rounding, a crewmember on *French Kiss*'s spinnaker pole – he has just released the red spinnaker flying off to the left – seems to dangle over the deck of *Heart of America*, the challenge candidate from Chicago, Illinois. The challenger fleet included two French and six U.S. boats.

Some of the most exciting racing was between *Stars & Stripes* (foreground) and *New Zealand* in the final challenger elimination series. The Kiwis had the best record in the early eliminations, but as the wind began to blow in December, *Stars & Stripes* took charge. In winds consistently stronger than 18 knots, Conner beat Chris Dickson 4-1.

At the end of a run, *New Zealand* roars down a wave as the spinnaker halyard shoots out on *Stars & Stripes*. In a moment, they will round a mark just to our right and commence banging their way back upwind through the steep chop. The Twelves were sailed like dinghies.

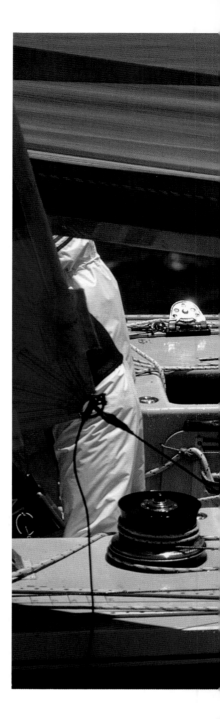

A jib-tailer in *Stars & Stripes* allows a small, personal celebration in the midst of her triumphant march by *New Zealand* and *Kookaburra III*. "Intense" is too weak a word for Conner's three-year campaign to win the Cup back.

Looking a bit dejected during their sweep by *Stars & Stripes*, the crew of the Australian defender *Kookaburra III* douses a jib.

At the start of the third race of the Cup match, on February 2, 1987, Iain Murray in *Kookaburra III* (left) has a slight advantage over *Stars & Stripes*. *Kookaburra* easily beat Alan Bond's *Australia IV* in her eliminations, but now Murray is down 0-2 against the master of 12-Meter match racing.

As the boats tacked back and forth over the next few minutes, the Australians seemed to gain a little. Conner kept attacking, hoping for a small wind shift, a burst of speed, or a mistake on the other boat. Judging by how far her jib is eased and by the activity of her crew, *Stars & Stripes* has just completed a tack and is going after the leading Aussies once again.

A moment later, *Kookaburra's* mainsail zipper (opened on downwind legs to make the sail more full) breaks. A man is hauled aloft to fix it. Soon he'll come down, the Aussies will tack, and *Stars & Stripes* will sail right by them to win the race by almost 2 minutes. Her back broken by this crushing defeat, *Kookaburra* lost the fourth race and the Cup two days later.

Stars & Stripes hightails it away from a mark
(off to the left) as *New Zealand* approaches. From a
distance, this would be one of those classic, majestic
pictures. But up this close, we feel the sting of spray
and sweat in the eyes of the winch-grinders as they
get in that last couple of inches.

(Left) Buxom but unsuccessful, the defense candidate *South Australia* pulls a little rooster tail as
she plows through a silvery sea at maximum speed.
The stream of water from her side is from her bilge
pump. A lot of Indian Ocean found its way aboard
during the Southern Hemisphere's summer of the
Twelves.

Her decks crowded with back-up crew, support staff, and friends, *Stars & Stripes* shows some stars and stripes as she sails to her welcome after winning the fourth and last race. Although the Australians would have been happier with a successful defense, Conner's victory was popular.

Having won back the Cup that he had lost 40 months earlier, Dennis Conner displays his prize. His accomplishment was extraordinary.

(Top) Dressed appropriately, the cheerleaders for *Stars & Stripes* watch from a spectator boat. In the foreground, the darkhaired woman in glasses just to the right of the woman with the hat is Judy Conner.

(Above) Waterfront celebrations have been known to bring out a wide range of enthusiasts. The dignified gentleman in the tuxedo with "Newport" on the lapel waits for the chance to present a bottle of champagne to the winners.

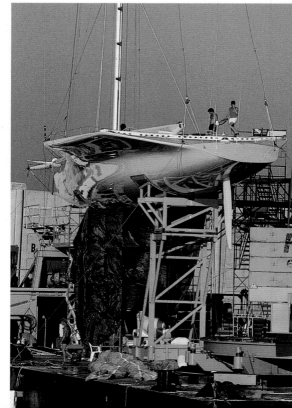

Highly competitive and drawn to challenges, New Zealand banker Michael Fay was especially effective in the public arena, where, of course, he often found himself in 1988.

Nothing like *New Zealand* had been built since *Ranger.* Here she is hauled out. Her 35-man crew sat out on her wings to provide stability and keep her sailing on her lines.

The San Diego Yacht Club and Conner's syndicate planned to have a great international gathering of 12-Meters at the next America's Cup, but they got bogged down over details. While they were distracted, New Zealander Michael Fay, whose *New Zealand* had done so well at Fremantle, challenged for the Cup not with a 12-Meter but with a huge sloop that harkened back to the Big Class. That was in July of 1987. San Diego refused the challenge, whereupon Fay appealed to the Supreme Court of the State of New York, which serves as guardian over the Cup's Deed of Gift. Justice Carmen B. Ciparick ruled in Fay's favor because of the Deed's concern about the right of a challenger to get a race. Obviously hoping to dispense with Fay's bothersome challenge as efficiently as possible, Conner and his backers responded by building a high-tech 60-foot catamaran that would make a short meal of any monohull, even the 120-foot *New Zealand*. The results of the races could be predicted accurately long before the starting gun. In all of Cup history, the ill will surrounding the two races of the 27th contest in 1988 were matched only by the rancor of the first one in 1870. Every other time, there was agreement about the fundamental principles of the competition.

(Left) Since the 1988 free-for-all ignored measurement rules, the designers were able to produce two extraordinary yachts. Conner's catamaran *Stars & Stripes* was a wing-masted wonder capable of sustaining speeds greater than 20 knots. Some of his crew were catamaran experts; others were trusted old hands from his 12-Meter days.

(Bottom) In a scene that reminded some of a political boss being protected by his hand-picked guards, Conner scowls during a pre-race press conference.

Doing at least 12 knots, *New Zealand* close-reaches in very little wind. She shared some dimensions with *Reliance* (page 40) and *Ranger* (page 57): a 90-foot waterline length; about 18,000 square feet of sail area; and a crew of 30 or more. The big difference, and a tribute to modern boatbuilding technology, was that she weighed only about 60,000 pounds – less than 20 percent the displacement of the big America's Cup contenders of the past.

Skipper David Barnes is somewhere in this crowd. The main winches are down below, as are a bank of computers connected to performance sensors all over the boat.

The mainsail floats off *New Zealand's* deck on the backs of 18 Kiwi crewmembers. Once again, there's no substitute for muscle power.

The real problem with the America's Cup in the 1980's was that some people were trying to wrench a freewheeling 19th-century event into the tightly scheduled, hyped-up media world of the late 20th century. America's Cup racing was designed to be — and until very recently was — an arena for people who take pleasure in challenging each other to outsized head-to-head contests. This is why it attracted such entrepreneurs and characters as John Cox Stevens, Thomas Lipton, Charlie Barr, Oliver Iselin, Thomas Sopwith, Harold Vanderbilt, Bus Mosbacher, and Alan Bond. Michael Fay was attracted in the same way. Fay may be infuriating, but he is a quintessential 19th-century man and the archetypal Cup figure. The question is whether he and the traditional approach to the America's Cup are anachronisms.

Part of the Kiwi crew runs across the leeward wing to lend a hand. The black lines are foam protrusions that are photographed by cameras aloft. The visual images are then converted into numerical data to help the crew optimize sail trim.

New Zealand crewmembers get their backs into bending on the 1000-pound mainsail. The luff slides are ball-bearing cars.

(Left) Stars & Stripes had her own wonders. She was the first Cup boat – in fact, one of the first racing yachts – to carry advertisements for commercial sponsors.

(Left) Conner and Barnes warily shake hands at one of their bitter press conferences as *New Zealand* designer Bruce Farr looks on thoughtfully. After the bizarre contest, Michael Fay went to court to ask that the catamaran be declared illegal. Six months later, on March 28, 1989, New York State Supreme Court Justice Carmen B. Ciparick disqualified *Stars & Stripes* for violating the Cup's Deed of Gift and the intentions of its donors. The San Diego Yacht Club then appealed the judge's ruling to a higher court, and it became anybody's guess when races would be held next.

(Right) Although she was sailed very conservatively in order to minimize the chance of damage, the catamaran won the two races by 18 and 21 minutes around a 40-mile course in the Pacific Ocean off San Diego.

New Zealand, a flashback to the glory days of the Big Class and the J's, approaches the finish of her doomed series, trailing the catamaran by several miles. Soon after, an international committee of yacht designers developed a new Cup class of speedy, telegenic 75-footers that will look like her. To many observers, this was one of many changes transforming the America's Cup, and not necessarily for the better. However, the Cup is resilient. As we have seen in these pages, during its long history Cup racing has survived many calamities to come back stronger and healthier than ever. Its historic appeal depends neither on controversy nor on the particular qualities of the yachts involved. What counts are the competitiveness inherent in the human spirit and the dreams and ambitions of energetic people eager to duel with each other in wind and water.

Brief Bibliography

Dear, Ian. *The America's Cup: An Informal History.* New York: Dodd, Mead, 1980.

— *Enterprise to Endeavour: The J-Class Yachts.* Revised Edition. London: Editors Inc., 1986.

Rosenfeld, Stanley. *A Century Under Sail.* Reading, Mass.: Addison-Wesley, 1984.

Rousmaniere, John. *America's Cup Book, 1851-1983.* New York: W. W. Norton, 1983.

— *The Golden Pastime: A New History of Yachting.* New York: W. W. Norton, 1986.

— *The Low Black Schooner: Yacht America, 1851-1945.* Mystic, Ct.: Mystic Seaport Museum Stores/W. W. Norton, 1987.

Thompson, Winfield M. and Thomas W. Lawson. *The Lawson History of the America's Cup.* Boston: Privately Published, 1902.

Vanderbilt, Harold S. *On the Wind's Highway.* New York: Scribner's, 1939.

Credits